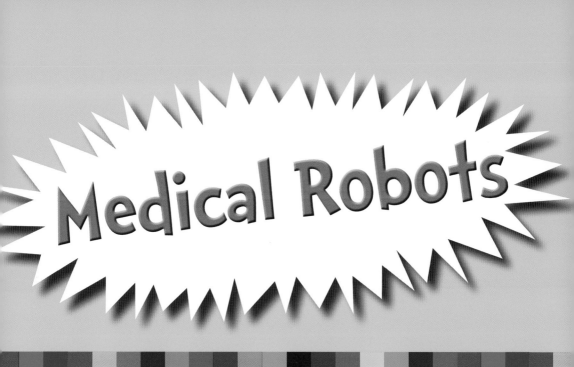

Medical Robots

BY NADIA HIGGINS

AMICUS HIGH INTEREST • AMICUS INK

Amicus High Interest and Amicus Ink are imprints of Amicus
P.O. Box 1329, Mankato, MN 56002
www.amicuspublishing.us

Library of Congress Cataloging-in-Publication Data
Names: Higgins, Nadia, author.
Title: Medical robots / by Nadia Higgins.
Description: Mankato, Minnesota : Amicus High Interest/
  Amicus Ink, [2018] | Series: Robotics in our world |
  Audience: Grades 4 to 6. | Includes bibliographical
  references and index.
Identifiers: LCCN 2016034045 (print) | LCCN 2016038294
  (ebook) | ISBN 9781681511436 (library binding) | ISBN
  9781681521749 (pbk.) | ISBN 9781681512334 (ebook)
  | ISBN 9781681512334 (pdf)
Subjects: LCSH: Robotics in medicine–Juvenile literature. |
  Robots–Juvenile literature. | Medical technology–Juvenile
  literature. | Medical innovations–Juvenile literature.
Classification: LCC R857.R63 H54 2018 (print) | LCC R857.
  R63 (ebook) | DDC 610.285/63–dc23
LC record available at https://lccn.loc.gov/2016034045

Editor: Wendy Dieker
Series Designer: Kathleen Petelinsek
Book Designer: Tracy Myers
Photo Researcher: Holly Young

Photo Credits: Stocktrek Images/Getty cover; Ed Stannard/
New Haven Register/AP 4-5; Hasbro/AP/REX/Shutterstock
6; Az Damiaan Oostende/AP/REX/Shutterstock 9; Erik
Möller/WikiCommons 10-11; NASA/Russell L. Schweickart/
WikiCommons 13; Roger Ressmeyer/Corbis/VCG/Getty 14;
Trax/ZUMA Press/Newscom 17; Noah Berger/Bloomberg/
Getty Images 18; Oliver Berg/dpa picture alliance/Alamy
Stock Photo 21; Victor Habbick Visions/Science Photo Library/
Newscom 22; JP5\ZOB/WENN/Newscom 25; Reuters/
Baz Ratner/Newscom 26; Kerim Okten/European Pressphoto
Agency B.V./Alamy Stock Photo 28-29

Printed in the United States of America

HC 10 9 8 7 6 5 4 3 2 1
PB 10 9 8 7 6 5 4 3 2 1

Table of Contents

A Robot Healer

Paro is waking up. He opens his eyes. He blinks. He shakes his whiskers. At a hospital, patients gather round. They pat Paro's head. They rub his nose. Paro coos, and they all laugh. This fuzzy seal pup has a special job. He makes patients feel better. Paro is a **therapy** robot.

Paro the robot seal cheers up a girl in the hospital.

A robot cat can make people just as happy as a real cat. But a robot is easier to care for.

 Do robots have feelings?

Therapy pets help people heal faster. But live animals are messy. They need a lot of care. So **engineers** invented robot pets. These machines have **sensors**. They can sense light, sound, and touch. They also have a computer inside. The sensors and computer let them react to your touches. Some can remember faces. Some will even come if you call them.

Not yet. But some robots can recognize expressions. They can copy human faces.

How are therapy robots different from a toy? Robots can move on their own. They can react to the world. They seem smart and almost human-like.

In hospitals, robots are busy. They are doing jobs to help patients, doctors, and nurses. Robots can bring blankets. They can count out pills. They are even doing surgery.

Pepper is a robot greeter at a hospital. It helps people learn where to go.

How Did We Get Here?

Can robots save lives? For ages, people have wondered. In the 1400s, Leonardo da Vinci drew plans for a robot knight. It wore armor. A crank made it go. It could move its head or wave. Could a robot like that ever take a person's place in battle?

People built a model based on da Vinci's drawings of a mechanical man.

11

People kept dreaming. They kept thinking. Along came electricity, computers, and plastics. In the 1900s, these three things advanced very quickly. So did robots.

By the 1960s, astronauts were flying into space. What if the astronauts got sick? Sending doctors would not do. Maybe robots could help out. Engineers got busy.

These astronauts were some of the first people in space. Could robots have helped them?

13

Dr. Yik San Kwoh shows how a robotic arm can help him do brain surgery.

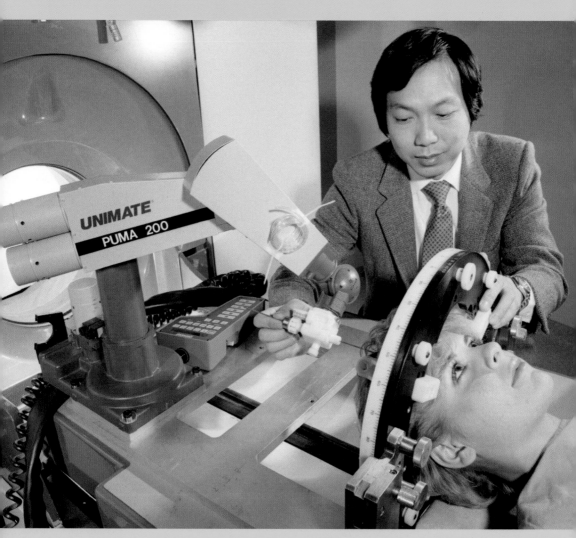

 How many operations do robots do each year?

By the 1980s, doctors were using robots to help during surgery. The robot could hold needles steady. It drilled neat holes into bone. Along came the da Vinci surgery robot. It was named after the great inventor. When doctors used robots to help, patients bled less. They healed faster. Robot doctors are not working in space yet. But they are saving lives on Earth!

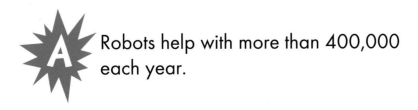 Robots help with more than 400,000 each year.

How Medical Robots Work

During surgery, the da Vinci robot sits by the patient. Its four arms easily reach over. Each one holds a tiny tool. One tool is a camera. It sends pictures to the screens. The doctor works behind one screen. He or she moves controls that move the robot arms. The doctor may move an inch. The robot arm moves a hair's width.

 **Q** Does the doctor have to be close by?

A doctor shows how the da Vinci's tools can move tiny items.

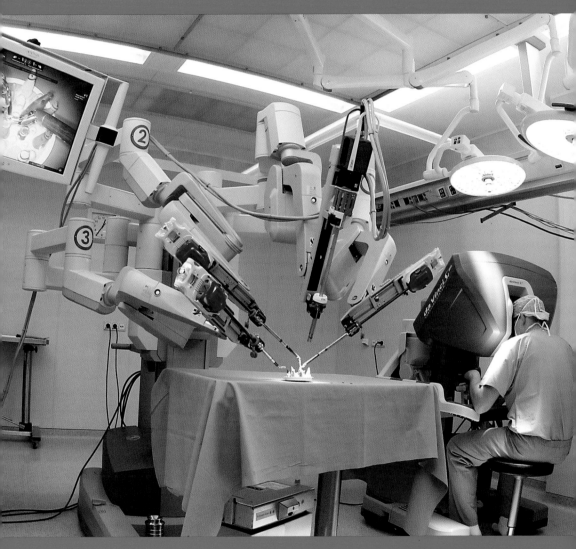

 No. With robots, doctors can work on patients across the ocean! And they have. Most of the time, the doctor is in the same room.

The TUG robot carries items around a hospital on its own.

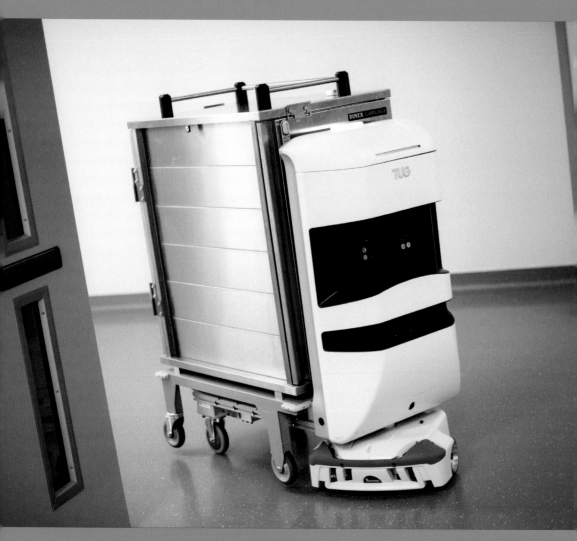

 Can TUG talk?

Meanwhile, a robot named TUG scoots all around hospital floors. This boxy robot can bring a meal. It can take out trash. It can carry medicine. First, a person loads TUG. Then they tap a touch screen to tell the robot where to go. TUG maps out its own route. It uses wi-fi to call elevators. Its sensors make sure it does not run into people.

 Yes. It says a few things. If you are in its way, it will say, "Please stand aside."

Robots also help doctors learn. Health workers need to learn to give shots. Dentists learn to drill teeth. They can practice on robots. Robots do not mind if the doctors-in-training make mistakes.

These robots seem like real humans. BabySIM can drool and cry. You can check its heartbeat. Pain Girl's teeth have sensors in them. She yelps when a dentist makes a wrong move.

 Can you kill a robot?

New dentists can learn how to give shots on Pain Girl. It acts like a real person.

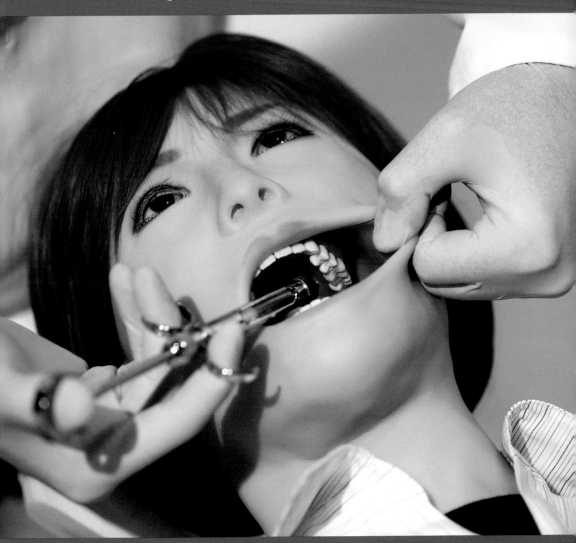

 Kind of. BabySIM can "die" if doctors really mess up. Luckily, the robot comes back to life.

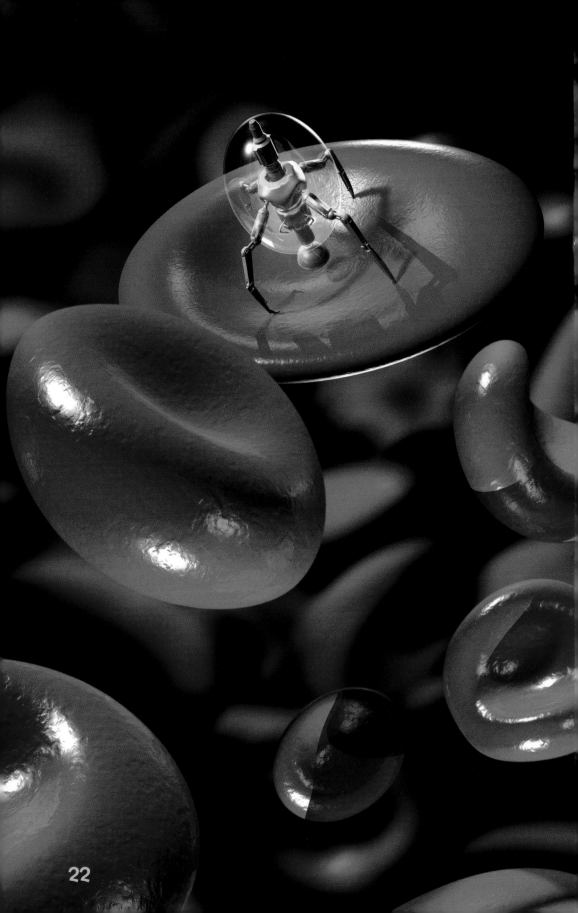

What Comes Next?

Imagine the smallest robots ever. You could swallow them in a pill. That is the idea behind **nanobots**. These tiny robots would travel through blood. They could carry medicine to a tumor or kill germs, one-on-one. How would these robots find their way? They could use the pull of magnets. They could ride with **bacteria**. Scientists are still figuring it out.

A drawing shows what a nanobot on a blood cell might look like.

Robotic body parts are another wave of the future. Some people already have **bionic** legs. These parts push and pull like real muscles. They can climb stairs. They can kick a ball.

Some robot legs use **artificial intelligence**. The legs can learn! The robot's computer notices how a person likes to walk. The leg responds. It angles just right to make each step seem natural.

A robotic ankle learns the best movements for its user. It automatically adjusts.

This ReWalk suit helps a paralyzed man walk again. Robotic parts help move his legs.

Exoskeletons strap on over the legs. These robot suits give power to people who cannot walk. Someday, the suits could replace wheelchairs.

The ReWalk suit includes a backpack with a battery. Metal crutches are just for balance. The person operates the suit through a wrist control. They press sit, stand, or walk. The robot kicks into action.

Amazing Robots

Bionic body parts attach to the skin. What if they could connect to the brain? Humans have already moved robot arms just by thinking. Medical robots already do many jobs in hospitals. They cheer people up. They help nurses and doctors. Doctors on earth don't do surgery in space yet, but scientists are working toward that. The future of machines in medicine is amazing!

Claire Lomas injured her spine. She can't walk on her own. The ReWalk robot helped her walk a marathon in 2012.

Glossary

artificial intelligence A robot's ability to learn and make choices on its own.

bacteria Microscopic creatures that live inside human bodies.

bionic Robotic in a way that copies the human body.

engineer Someone who designs and builds things, such as robots.

exoskeleton A robot suit that uses robotic technology to help a person move.

nanobot A tiny robot that is as small as the cells in a person's body.

sensor A robot part that can detect light, sound, or other things that we detect with our five senses.

therapy Having to do with exercises, devices or processes that help with healing.

Read More

Hayes, Susan and Tory Gordon-Harris. *Really? Robots*. New York: Scholastic Inc., 2015.

McCollum, Sean. *The Fascinating, Fantastic, Unusual History of Robots*. Mankato, Minn.: Capstone Press, 2012.

Stewart, Melissa. *Robots*. Washington, D.C.: National Geographic, 2014.

Websites

FIRST Robotics Competition
http://www.firstinspires.org/robotics/frc

Robots for Kids
http://www.sciencekids.co.nz/robots.html

Tobey's Robot Workshop
http://pbskids.org/wordgirl/games/robotworkshop/

Index

About the Author

Nadia Higgins is the author of more than 100 books for children and young adults. She has written about everything from ants to zombies, with many science and technology topics in between. Higgins lives in Minneapolis, Minnesota, with her human family, pet lizard, and robotic dog.